The Way and The Word

The Tao of Jesus

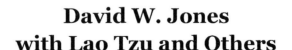

**David W. Jones
with Lao Tzu and Others**

David W. Jones
Valjean Press, Nashville

Introduction

A friend asked me if I believe Jesus is the way, the truth, and the life (John 14). I replied, "Of course." As a pastor, a professional Christian, it is an easy question. I placed my bet a long time ago. Even for amateur Christians, the question is simple. All it asks of us is, "What do you believe about Jesus?"

The question is by nature exclusive. If Jesus is The Way, then all others are ruled out. Mohammed, Buddha, Krishna, you get one vote and one vote only. Join a church, or simply attend worship service, you'll be asked to affirm who Jesus is above all others. You might unite with the congregation professing the divine nature of Jesus using words from the fourth century's Nicene Creed,

> *(Jesus is) the only-begotten Son of God, begotten of the Father before all ages, God of God, Light of Light, very God of very God, begotten not made, being of one substance with the Father...*

Perhaps, at the same worship service, you'll hear read the words of Jesus from John 10 where he speaks of his own identity, "I and the Father are One," or from the first verses of John's gospel that profess Jesus as The Word, One with God,

> *In the beginning was the Word, and the Word was with God, and the Word was God. (Jesus) was in the beginning with God. All things came into being through him, and without him not one thing came into being. What has come into being in him was life, and the life was*

the light of all people. The light shines in the darkness, and the darkness did not overcome it.

My struggle, as I start my fourth decade in ministry, is simple. Somewhere along the journey from one millennia to another, I believe we have over focused on our professions and neglected our practices. I wonder if Jesus' first disciples would even recognize us today as fellow followers of Jesus if they showed up to worship on a Sunday or in our homes on Monday. When Jesus taught his first followers, he recognized his way held a higher standard than the way they had been instructed throughout their lives. Here are selections from The Sermon on The Mount (Matthew 5-7),

> Matthew 5: *21 "You have heard that it was said to those of ancient times, 'You shall not murder'; and 'whoever murders shall be liable to judgment.' 22 But I say to you that if you are angry with a brother or sister, you will be liable to judgment; and if you insult a brother or sister, you will be liable to the council; and if you say, 'You fool,' you will be liable to the hell of fire.*

> Matthew 5: *27 "You have heard that it was said, 'You shall not commit adultery.' 28 But I say to you that everyone who looks at a woman with lust has already committed adultery with her in his heart.*

> Matthew 5: *38 "You have heard that it was said, 'An eye for an eye and a tooth for a tooth.' 39 But I say to you, Do not resist an evildoer. But if anyone strikes you on the right*

cheek, turn the other also; [40] and if anyone wants to sue you and take your coat, give your cloak as well; [41] and if anyone forces you to go one mile, go also the second mile. [42] Give to everyone who begs from you, and do not refuse anyone who wants to borrow from you.

Matthew 5: [43] *"You have heard that it was said, 'You shall love your neighbor and hate your enemy.' [44] But I say to you, Love your enemies and pray for those who persecute you, [45] so that you may be children of your Father in heaven; for he makes his sun rise on the evil and on the good, and sends rain on the righteous and on the unrighteous. [46] For if you love those who love you, what reward do you have? Do not even the tax collectors do the same? [47] And if you greet only your brothers and sisters, what more are you doing than others?*

The contrast of Jesus' way to other ways has remained distinct. For example, most religions have a "Golden Rule." Though often unnoticed, Jesus' version is significantly different from all others. See if you notice Jesus' variation. I listed Jesus' version first.

Do to others as you would have them do to you.
Luke 6:31

Do not do to others what you would not like yourself.
Then there will be no resentment against you,
either in the family or in the state.
Confucius, Analects 12:2

5

Hurt not others in ways that you yourself
would find hurtful.
Buddha, Udana-Varga 5,1

This is the sum of duty;
do naught unto others
what you would not have them
do unto you.
Hinduism, Mahabharata 5,1517

The definitive difference is that the other "Golden Rules" are cited in the negative. "Do not do to others what you do not want done to you." Jesus' version is in the affirmative requiring doing to others as you want others to do for you. This is a big step from just not doing to others what you don't want done unto you. For Jesus, 'others' include both our family, friends, and allies as well as the stranger, the foreigner, and those who consider us to be their enemies. That is Jesus' way.

When Jesus declared himself to be The Way, Jesus' followers were to adopt his way as their way as all disciples do. Over time, as the church became institutionalized, professing Jesus without practicing Jesus, Christians, , became less Christ-like taking their roles as cheerleaders and chaplains for the status quo. We preach Jesus' Way as some far off goal that God never really wanted us to follow, like setting your alarm ten minutes early when you know you'll only press the snooze button. We praise Jesus, pray to him, but follow him? Walk in his way? Embody The Way? Let me just hit that snooze button one more time.

Granted, The Way is difficult. That's why Paul calls the gospel foolish at its core (1 Corinthians). Absurd though it may be, it is not near as absurd as separating belief in Jesus as The Way from living his way altogether. We may be blind to the absurdity, others are not as Kurt Vonnegut observed,

> *For some reason, the most vocal Christians among us never mention the Beatitudes (Matthew 5). But, often with tears in their eyes, they demand that the Ten Commandments be posted in public buildings. And of course, that's Moses, not Jesus. I haven't heard one of them demand that the Sermon on the Mount, the Beatitudes, be posted anywhere. "Blessed are the merciful" in a courtroom? "Blessed are the peacemakers" in the Pentagon? Give me a break!"*

While in our safe sanctuaries we may profess Jesus as The Way while it's obvious to everyone else that we casted it off long ago in favor of more 'realistic' mantras, like this one – *the ends justify the means.* For Jesus, the ends never justified the means, no matter how good the goal. For Jesus, the means were the end. That was and is his way. You love because you love, it's your way, even if it gets you crucified. You don't judge, condemn, or treat others with contempt, apparently even in the midst of a crucifixion, because that's not your way. You help the least of these precisely because, in God's eyes, we are all children, and none among us, no matter how destitute, are "least." That was Jesus' way and clearly his intent to be the way of his followers. The ends don't justify the means, the means are the end. That was and is to be our way.

7

Can a pianist be separated from daily practice? Can an athlete be dissected from years of work and ongoing training? Can a recovering addict be separated from the 12 Steps? Certainly not. They are constantly on the path to becoming. So, too, with followers of Jesus, to join on the journey, The Word and The Way are One. So, if we are going to follow the Word, then we must walk in The Way. As many have said, being fans is not enough. We must become followers, walking in The Way. If we are going to truly proclaim Jesus as "The Way, The Truth, and The Life," then we must live, practice, and embody that Way, Truth, and Life in our own ways, truths, and lives and not just as a holy footnote to our own ways and our own words. Sooner or later, like the wise magi of old, we'll have to set our direction back to the star light and realign our compass with true North, Jesus' Way.

What does Jesus' Way look like? Recently, as I will share in the pages that follow, I have found inspiration in a philosopher that lived long before Jesus named Lao Tzu, which means "The Ol' Boy," a nickname with which a southerner like me can identify. As I've read and reread his work, I've found him to be quite a "Good Ol' Boy" and I have learned much.

As therapists often say, "The last animal to discover water was a fish." Which means, if you want to learn about your family, perhaps you need to talk to someone with an outside perspective. This is what I've found, an outside perspective in *The Tao*, or simply translated into English, *The Way*, authored by Lao Tzu, whose name is often translated as "Old Child."

This Good Ol' Boy lived long before states were united in America or there was an America, long before Britain was an empire, and even a good five centuries before Jesus. Apparently, neither he nor Jesus were big on writing things down, and as legend has it, as Lao Tzu was about to leave the country, a border guard said, "But what about your teachings? How will we know The Way when you're gone?" Lao Tzu saw the concern in his face and wrote *The Tao.*

The Chinese word for *Tao,* pronounced *Dow,* combines the symbols for *walking,* which shows a person traveling down a road, and *mind* which symbolizes the dual power of the brain to store information and imagine new possibilities. The symbol has an internal organizing structure, almost like a filing cabinet, and has sparks of inspiration arising out of the top. What is the *Tao?* It is a *mind walking,* thinking and doing, professing and practicing. *The Tao* unifies thought and action in an inseparable fashion as the author of the biblical book of James would centuries later. *The Tao* recognizes, as did many biblical writers, right thinking can lead to right doing (orthodoxy), but even more so, right practice leads to right thinking (orthopraxis).

As I read and reread *The Tao,* I used many translations, though I have referred to Stephen Mitchell's version the most. Like a fish out of water looking back from whence I came, I see Jesus' Way in a broader perspective hearing *The Tao* throughout

The New Testament, especially in *Matthew, Mark, Luke, John,* and the non-canonical *Gospel of Thomas.*

The following pages are what happened when I let Jesus and Lao Tzu sing a duet while I listened for the harmonies. This work is not a translation or a paraphrase of *The Gospels* or *The Tao,* but instead a blended format with a revolutionary goal, to reunite Jesus, The Word, with Jesus, The Way in hopes that we will spiritually ascend to where he's been calling us to go for 2,000 years, embodying The Way, The Truth, and The Life.

Respectfully Submitted,

David W. Jones
2017

Preparation

Search me, O God.
Know my heart, my thoughts, and my actions.
Keep me from any wicked ways,
and lead me in The Way everlasting. Psalm 139:23-24

If you want to live fully
then lay aside immaturity
and walk in The Way. Proverbs 9:6

Listen, my child, and be wise.
Direct your mind in The Way. Proverbs 23:19

I am God. I will teach you for your own good.
I will lead you in The Way. Isaiah 48:17

Have you not realized so much of your pain
you have brought upon yourself
by turning aside from God and The Way? Jeremiah 2:17

Thomas said to him, "Lord...
How can we know the way?"
Jesus said to him, "I am The Way..." John 14:5-6

In the beginning was The Word... John 1:1

One

Shhhh...
   The Way cannot be spoken.
   You can only point.

Become quiet.
   If you speak, only whisper
   for The Way is beyond words.

Become still.
   If you think, don't think too much.
   The Way cannot be bound by your beliefs.

Become calm.
   Let your mind relax.
   Allow the waters of your soul to settle.

Become open.
   Don't strive after certainty,
   or you will be blinded by your own illusions.
   Instead, let go of what you think you know.
   Open yourself to mystery,
   for The Way is greater than your imagination.

Two

Beware of categories.
 As soon as you label something as 'beautiful,'
 you will begin to see 'ugly.'
 Call some 'better,'
 and you will define others as 'worth-less.'
 Draw a circle around 'us,'
 and you'll see others as 'them.'
 Build a wall to create 'insiders,'
 and you will continue to cast more and more
 over your walls until none are left,
 except you alone.

Beware of polarizing dualities.
 'Difficult' fashions 'easy.'
 'Long' forms 'short.'
 'Up' tops 'down.'
 'High' necessitates 'low.'
 'After' surges ahead of 'before.'
 'Sooner' cuts in front of 'later.'
 'Winning' must outscore 'losing.'
 'Success' must frown upon 'failure.'
 Each needs the other,
 like 'richer' needs 'poorer,'
 'right' needs 'wrong,'
 or neither can exist.

All are only fabrications.
Languages and labels never last.
Only The Unnamable is forever real.

Three

Over value your own ability,
*   and you will foster the people around you*
*   to become feeble and dependent.*
*   Raise the famous to a pedestal,*
*   and you will create dictators.*
*   Treat people like objects,*
*   and you will find yourself objectified.*
*   Lock away your treasures,*
*   and you will invite thieves.*

When you lose your toys and don't weep,
*   or when you don't get your way and don't wail,*
*   not only will you be an adult,*
*   but you'll be walking in The Way.*

Take the low seat, and wait for someone
*   to come and raise you up.*
*   If no one comes, wait for a while longer.*
*   If no one still comes, then get up and go about your life.*
*   The Way is more than silly games*
*   of high and low, good seats and bad seats,*
*   honour and dishonour by others.*
*   Honour is your choice,*
*   no one can bestow it upon you,*
*   nor take it away.*
*   That is The Way.*

Four

The word that can be spoken is not the eternal Word.
The path that can be mapped is not the eternal Path.
The light that succumbs to shadows is not the eternal Light.

The truth that can be told is not the eternal Truth.
The life that ends is not the eternal Life.
The way that can be written is not the eternal Way.

The Way is the well that never runs dry.
   The Way is the pantry that is never empty.
   The Way is the bread that continually satisfies.
   The Way is the wine, which, when you drink it,
   you become more and more sober.

Never seen but always visible,
   silent but always speaking,
   boundless yet always within reach,
   that is The Way.

Five

People create divisions, but The Way transcends borders.

Why do you use a telescope to see
*   another's faults from far away,*
*   or a microscope to scrutinize*
*   another's failings in great detail,*
*   when you haven't examined*
*   your own flaws at all?*

Judge another, and you judge yourself.
*   Show contempt for another,*
*   and you reveal your self-contempt.*
*   Hate another, and you show your self-hate.*
*   To accept others, accept yourself.*
*   To give another grace, give yourself grace.*
*   To love another, love yourself.*
*   Do you think God has self-image problems?*
*   Then why should you, created in the image of God,*
*   worry about your self-worth?*

When you think you have no value, remember this story,
*   God's kingdom is like a jeweller searching for a fine pearl.*
*   When he found it, he rejoiced, sold all he had and bought it.*
*   God is the jeweller. You are the pearl.*
*   For God to sell all for you is no sacrifice.*
*   That's how valuable you are to God.*
*   That's the way God is. That's the way love is.*
*   That is The Way.*

Six

The Way is like the sower scattering seed everywhere.
    Some falls upon the road eaten by the birds.
    Some falls upon rocks and never takes root.
    Some falls upon thorns and are choked out.
    Some falls upon the good soil and brings forth a healthy crop.
    The sower is not concerned for seed that is lost.
    He does not worry about seed that is eaten by birds,
    that takes no root upon rocks, or is choked out by thorns.
    The sower understands life.
    Life grows exponentially.
    Life always wins over roads, rocks, and thorns.
    So it is with The Way.

The Way is like a mustard seed tiny but large in life.
The Way is like kudzu, once it starts growing in your field,
    you'll never get it out.
The Way is like yeast, a small amount does much
    transforming a lump of dough into a loaf,
    and all who eat of it are filled.

Seven

The Way was in the beginning, never born,
  always was, always is, always will be.

The Way is spacious, without boundary,
  wall, fence, or gate,
  present for all,
  without desire for itself.

Be careful when you pray
  and ask God for a blessing.
  God might surprise you,
  giving you something you don't expect,
  like a cross.
  God's blessings are like that,
  sometimes even,
  sometimes uneven,
  and sometimes God's blessings
  are even odd.

Trust the secrets of The Way:
  stay behind to get ahead
  lose to win,
  fail to achieve,
  fall to rise
  die to live,
  pick up your cross,
  to discover your crown.
  That is The Way

Eight

The Way is like water.
  It nourishes all things,
  without effort or attempt.
  Willingly, it flows
  to the low places,
  freely it nurtures others
  without question or thought.

Like water, live grounded,
  think in simple ways,
  take shape in situations as needed,
  but do not become the container.

Though storms may rage
  around you,
  above you,
  over you,
  be still and calm,
  one with the sea,
  the deeper you go,
  the calmer you will become.

Nine

Can you drink the cup of your life fully?

Can you step back from your thoughts and see clearly?

Can you let your body relax like a born again child?

Can you feel your emotions without becoming your emotions?

Can you cast out the clutter from your mind
to see the light beyond the shadows?

Can you love and lead without dominating?

Can you turn aside to whatever thrones you might be offered
in order to be the servant of all?

Can you pick up your burdens and carry them fully,
letting The Way run its course in every place and time?

Ten

Fill your cup to the top, and it will spill.
Over sharpen your knife, you will make it dull.
Clench your fist around gold, and you'll get a heart attack.
Seek safety above all else, and you'll never feel secure.
Care about people's approval,
and you'll be a slave to opinions.
Think too much, and you'll go insane.

There are two great fears:
The fear of death and the fear of life.
When you are afraid of both life and death,
beginnings and endings,
slavery and freedom,
you will worry constantly.

The lamp of your mind is your eye.
If your eye has a cataract,
how can you see?
The interpreter for your eyes is your mind.
If your mind has a cataract,
how can you perceive?
Worry is like a mental cataract.
So, why worry?

Worry won't make tomorrow come quicker.
Worry won't fix your broken yesterday.
Worry won't keep you from squandering each moment.
So, why worry?

Worry won't feed you.
  Worry won't keep you safe.
  Worry won't make you live longer.
  So, why worry?

Why worry about your house
  when the world is your home?
  Why do you worry about death
  when you have yet to fully live?

Those who worry are
  like the group of starving people
  who asked God for beans.
  God gave them a banquet.
  They complained,
  "But where are our beans?"
  They were in the way
  but not in The Way.

Do you think the bird worries
  about what it will eat
  or what it will wear?
  Of course not!
  It's too busy flying.
  If it starts worrying, it will crash.
  Birds in flight are flying in The Way.
  Do likewise, or you'll crash.

Eleven

Accept your emptiness
*   like the wagon wheel,*
*   the center hole,*
*   the middle void,*
*   makes movement possible.*

Be like a clay pot,
*   let your emptiness*
*   be for the use of all.*

Be like a house,
*   with room between the walls*
*   that makes life for others possible.*

Be like music,
*   give space between the notes*
*   to turn sounds into a song.*

When you find you are without,
*   look to the empty space,*
*   explore the void within,*
*   there you will find The Way.*

Only one whose stomach is empty
*   can be filled.*
*   Only a soul that is hungry*
*   can be fed by The Way.*

Twelve

Beware of bright colors that can blind you,
loud noises that deafen you,
flavors that overpower your mouth,
thoughts that weaken your mind,
and desires that turn your heart to a desert.

Seek until you find.
When you find, you may be troubled.
If you can live through your trouble,
you will be astounded,
beyond your astonishment,
you will be enlightened.
The Way is not what you expect,
but far greater.

Be inner directed while outwardly focused.
Allow life to come and go,
accept every experience as a gift,
keep your heart as open as the sky.

Look for the eternal One while you live
trusting that when you die
the eternal One
will be
looking
for
you.

Thirteen

Winning and losing can both be fatal.
Success and failure can both be tragic.

For those climbing the ladder of success,
    ascending or descending,
    all positions are shaky.

Keep your balance by staying rooted to the earth.

Rain falls on the just and the unjust,
    the kind and the cruel,
    the compassionate and the heartless,
    all the same.
    So when it rains on your parade,
    don't take it personally.
    Accept the rain as simply weather on a given day,
    and you my friend, are not far from walking in The Way.

Fourteen

Squint, and you will not see.
Spy, and you will not observe.
Swipe, and you will never grasp.

Above is not brighter.
Below is not darker.
The Way is seamless.

The Way is being that welcomes nonbeing,
*   order that welcomes chaos,*
*   good encompasses evil,*
*   form that has no form,*
*   image without an image,*
*   simple beyond comprehension.*

Look back, there is no beginning.
*   Look ahead, there is no end.*
*   Look up, there is no top.*
*   Look below, there is no bottom.*
*   That is The Way.*

The Way is all around you.
*   Open your eyes and you will see it.*
*   Open your ears and you will hear it.*
*   Greet your neighbour,*
*   and you will find God among you.*

Fifteen

The wise have always been profound in simple ways.
  To describe what they were is not possible.
  Instead, speak about how they were.
  Not the people as your idol,
  but the way they lived as your goal.

The wise live cautiously
  careful as a person walking on rocks in a stream,
  alert like a deer with hunters close,
  hospitable to experiences and people
  like a host with honoured guests.

Like water, the wise are fluid.
Like a block of wood, they are shapeable.
Like a valley, they are receptive to whatever falls.
Like clean glass, they are clear.
Be likewise.

Sixteen

When you label others, you make it difficult to love others.
When you label experiences, calling the painful ones 'bad'
   and the pleasing ones 'good,'
   then you experience little but frustration.
   Let go of your expectations.

Cease thinking, empty your mind,
   let your heart settle on peace,
   watch the turmoil of others,
   but be confident
   as they spin away from you,
   they will return.

All life is from God.
All life returns to God.
Each separate being returns to the common source.
Returning is serine. Spinning is chaos.
Know the source, or stumble in confusion.
   Accept life as a little child,
   drenched in wonder,
   open to whatever life brings,
   and when death comes,
   you will be prepared.

If you live well, you'll be able to die well.
If you are prepared to die well,
   living well will become your way.

Seventeen

When you lead in The Way, people will hardly notice you.

The ends will not justify your means,
    as a walker of The Way
    the means will be your end.
    The Way will guide your actions.
    Your path will unfold.
    Your character will guide your steps
    as a compass guides a ship.

You will not need to control others or situations.
    You will claim your power to choose
    and help others do the same.

You will say little and accomplish much,
    and when goals are completed,
    the public will say, "Look at all we accomplished!"
    and when you arrive at your destination,
    all those who travel with you will say, "Look! We made it!"

Eighteen

Families seek constancy over health.
Congregations seek tradition over transformation.
Communities seek similarity over diversity.
Nations seek stability over justice.
People seek familiarity over peace.
Which is why few people grow in The Way,
they would rather stay the same for generations.

Ignore The Way,
and you'll be stuck in righteousness and ritual.
Ignore what is obvious,
and you'll be lost in certainty.
Ignore harmony in the family,
and you'll be bound by unquestionable loyalty.
Ignore the freedom of the people,
and the nation will fall into mindless patriotism.
Ignore the responsibility of the individual,
and the nation will be populated with narcissists.

The crowd travels the easy highway.
Do not go there simply because others do.
For all you know, they may be walking in the paths of cows.
Instead, follow The Way, even if it means a ninety degree turn
from the highway to the forest.
The path of The Way often winds into the wild.
Where else can you find an exciting adventure?

Nineteen

Children came to the scholars to learn The Way.
The teachers sent them away saying, "This is not for you.
"This is far too important and difficult for you to learn."
The teachers continued to talk, write,
and lecture about The Way,
but The Way
was nowhere
to be found.
The Way
was out
climbing
trees with
the children.

Does The Way sound foolish to you?
Then you have grown too old to grow.
If you want to know The Way, go ask a child.
He or she may reveal to you the secrets of the universe,
and all it might cost you is a cookie.

Twenty

Stop over thinking, and your problems will disappear.
* Why must everything be divided between yes and no,*
* success and failure, triumph and tragedy?*

Why must you value what others value,
* and avoid what others avoid?*
* How ridiculous!*

Why be excited just because others are excited,
* as though they were at a carnival?*

Be the alternative, unmoved by pageantry.
* Like a newborn, let the world be your festival.*

When others are bright, don't fear being dark.
When others are sharp, don't avoid being dull.
When others have a purpose, be uncertain.
When other people grasp and grab;
* go into the world with an open hand,*
* wander about, at home without a house,*
* like a happy fool let your mind be open,*
* and see the joke in everything.*

Float as on the ocean,
* adrift like a leaf in power of the wind,*
* the world is your home, the universe your country,*
* gravity is your only law.*

Twenty-One

Keep your mind in The Way and radiate.
Even though The Way is ungraspable,
*   you can find it by not clinging to ideas.*
Even though the path ahead may be dark,
*   The Way can glow in front of you because you let it.*

Beyond time and space,
*   beyond is and is not,*
*   beyond right and askew,*
*   is The Way.*

The truth that binds is not the eternal Truth.
*   The eternal Truth sets you free,*
*   points you to the right paths,*
*   not a degree you achieve,*
*   or a formula you can apply,*
*   but a direction you can follow.*
*   As a compass always points to True North,*
*   let your heart point to The Way,*
*   and then, even when you have no idea where you are,*
*   the course you are to travel will be clear.*
*   Your choice will be obvious.*
*   Your direction sure.*

Twenty-Two

Live in The Way and...
In partiality, you will find wholeness.
In the crooked, you will find straight.
In emptiness, you will find contentment.
In dying, you will find new life.
Once you've lost everything,
imagine what you'll discover.

Don't be like the rich man
who buried his wealth in the ground.
It didn't grow, and neither did he.
Many years later, he was planted
in the earth right beside the spot
where he hid his wealth,
and there he decayed
right along with it.

Why do you keep looking in poison ivy
trying to find spinach?
Why do you reach into a bramble of thorns
and expect to pull out a handful of berries?
Know trees by their fruit.
Know thorns by your scars.

When you see a group not living The Way,
become a passer-by.
Why gain the whole world and lose your soul
when you can gain all by letting everything go?

Twenty-Three

Speak, then hush.

Be like nature,
    the wind blows,
    then is silent,
    the rain falls,
    then is still.

Open yourself to The Way,
    and you can embody it completely.

Open yourself to The Truth,
    and you can express it clearly.

Open yourself to The Life,
    and minutes will disappear as moments take their place.

Walk in The Way and become The Way.
Embody The Truth and become True.
Live The Life and come Alive.

When you eat, eat.
    When you sleep, sleep.
    When you walk, walk.
    When you sit, relax.
    That is The Way.

Twenty-Four

Stand on your toes and you will tip over.
Rush ahead and you'll be left behind.
Try to be famous, and you'll disappear completely.

Live out the labels of others,
   no matter your title,
   you'll never be certain of who you are.

Try to control others,
   they will have power over you,
   and you'll lose your self-control.

Make your job your life's purpose,
   little you do will last.

Try to leave a legacy,
   your legacy will leave you.

To be One with The Way,
   do your work,
   live your purpose,
   let it pass from
   your hands to God's,
   and anything will be possible.

Twenty-Five

In the beginning was The Word.
    Unchanging.
    Infinite.
    The source of all that was to come.

From The Word comes The Way.
    The Word and The Way are One.

The Word and The Way are solitary and yet interwoven.
    The Word and The Way are
    unchanging and yet constantly adapting,
    eternally present and yet found in a moment.

The Way teaches in parables,
    once you are totally confused,
    and find yourself at a dead-end street,
    then The Way forward will be clear.
    One plus one equals elephant.
    That's how The Way works.

Keep your eyes open, pay attention, and look.
    The mysteries of The Way will be revealed in front of you.
    Nothing that is hidden won't be exposed.
    Nothing that is covered up won't be uncovered.
    The best eyes see.
    The best ears hear.
    So, look and listen.
    The Way is all around you.

Twenty-Six

The unmoved is the source of the moveable
The unnameable is the source of the nameable.

Praise those who curse you.
 If someone tries to steal your coat, give it to him gladly.
 If someone classifies you as "enemy", reject their label.
 If someone hates you, love them.
 When you give to someone, give freely,
 and do not keep a ledger expecting something in return.
 Why? Because you can. That's the power of The Way.

If someone strikes you, you do not have to strike back,
 you can always choose.
 If someone wrongs you,
 you do not have to wrong them in return,
 you can always choose.
 No matter what evil someone does to you,
 you do not have to repay evil for evil, violence for violence,
 wrongdoing with an even greater wrongdoing.
 No one ever forces your response,
 you can always choose.
 Why? Because you can. That's the power of The Way.

War never brings peace.
 Hate never produces love.
 Only liberated people who choose
 can dream the world into a new reality.
 That has always been The Way.

Twenty-Seven

If someone says, "The Way is only here,"
    and another says, "The Way is only there,"
    do not pay them any attention.
    No matter how loud they sing
    or what they promise,
    The Way is where it wills,
    anywhere and everywhere
    both here and there
    at the same time.

Travel with those who love a journey,
    accompany those who enjoy adventure,
    be a companion to those who laugh often.

If you heart is like a house with no door,
    how can you ever feel at home with anyone?
    If your heart is open, you can be at home
    with anyone, everywhere.

The people of The Way are never lost
    because they are always at home,
    no matter where they are.

Be like eagles,
    why care where your nest is,
    when your home is the sky?

Twenty-Eight

One day, God took The Way
and cooked it in a loaf of bread.
No one tasted it because
though they discussed the loaf,
they never took a bite.
As a result, all remained hungry and hornary.

If you come to The Way
expecting reward or punishment,
you will be disappointed,
they are not in The Way.

The one who is high, God will bring low.
The one who is low, God will raise up.
That's how God works.
Just ask Moses and Pharaoh.
The Way sees both rising and falling
as a potential blessing.

.

Twenty-Nine

The world was created 'good,'
*   so why do you want to improve it?*
*   Progress is a fairy tale.*

The world has a rhythm.
*   Walk in cadence.*
*   Move in time with the music.*

The world is alive, live in it.
*   Misuse the earth like an object,*
*   you'll die prematurely.*

The world is sacred space, holy ground,
*   take off your shoes,*
*   be present.*

Are you aware of what time it is?
*   Is it time for going ahead,*
*   or time for falling behind?*
*   Is it time for being in motion,*
*   or time for being at rest?*
*   Is it time to run vigorously,*
*   or time to fall exhausted?*
*   Is it time to seek safety,*
*   or time to take a risk?*
*   The answer to all these questions is, "Yes."*
*   Now is the time.*
*   The time is now.*

Thirty

If you are to lead others,
rely on The Way,
don't force issues,
or try to annihilate enemies.
For every force
there is a counterforce.
Violence always
rebounds on itself
no matter how well intended.

The one leading in The Way
does her job then stops,
understanding that the universe
is forever beyond her grasp.
She understands that trying
to dominate events is futile,
like grasping at the wind.
Instead she breathes,
trusting the life inside herself.

She has no need to convince or convert others,
that goes against the grain of The Way.

Content in The Way, trusting in life,
she doesn't need others' approval.
She accepts. The whole world can only accept her,
because she does not receive any other response.

Thirty-One

Weapons are violent tools,
the wise reject them.
Weapons are fearful tools,
the wise avoid them.

Hold peace as the highest value.
Without true peace
there can be no contentment.
There are no enemies, only people.
To wish personal harm on
the one seeking to be your enemy
accepts their delusions as your reality.

Understand others, and you are smart.
Understand yourself, and you'll be wise.

Control others, and you are strong.
Master yourself, and you will be truly powerful.

Thirty-Two

The Way is immeasurable,
    as small as an electron,
    as vast as a galaxy.

If you are in a position of power,
    remain centered in The Way,
    all things will harmonize,
    your world will be a paradise,
    your people will be at peace,
    the law will live in their hearts.

See labels for the formless images they are.
    See each institution for the function it serves
    not as an entity unto itself.

As rivers flow into the ocean, all life moves in The Way,
    you can flow with the current or resist it.
    The journey and destination are the same,
    though you'll experience them differently.
    Flow with The Way, and experience the joy of life's journey.
    Swim against The Way, every breath will be a struggle.

Thirty-Three

You have ears, why don't you listen?
  You have eyes, why can't you see?
  The Way is all around you,
  look, listen, taste, see, feel,
  there is The Way.

The Way is like the universe
  an empty void that provides room
  for infinite possibilities.
  Sound comes from silence.
  Light comes from darkness.
  Questions come from answers.
  From the address beyond coordinates,
  from the time beyond clocks that tic and toc,
  The Way enters the here and now.

When you worry about your life's end,
  stand at the beginning.
  The one who can stand at the beginning,
  doesn't worry about life's endings.

Thirty-Four

Like Adam and Eve,
God has given you the world as your garden paradise.
If you choose to eat from the forbidden fruit
in order to label everyone and every experience 'good' or 'ill,'
you will turn your heaven into a hell, just as they did.

People of The Way see beyond dualities and polarities.
Tuesday' is not the opposite of 'Thursday.'
'Left' does not oppose 'right.'
Both work together,
like eyes in the body,
exposed to one common light.
Yellow and Blue can live together in harmony
without arguing, fighting, or quarrelling,
they can collaborate and cooperate creating
something fresh, something new, something green.

Thirty-Five

Accept the human, but learn from the animal.
Ask a cat if it had a good day,
and it will not respond.
Cats have no concept of 'good' or 'bad.'
They just have days.
Learn from cats.

When the sun rises and sets,
when the tide approaches and withdraws,
in flood and drought
never labelling, always celebrating
fully experiencing each day
unfettered by expectations
welcoming each moment as it comes
releasing each moment as it goes
touching eternity.
That is The Way.

Thirty-Six

The gentle can overwhelm the rigid.

If you cast a stone at another,
    fire will come from it and devour your heart.
    If you speak against another,
    your words will consume you.
    All you will know is weeping and gnashing of teeth.
    The Way will not be in you.

Commandments come from commanders.
    Rules come from rulers.
    Freedom comes from The Way.
    Don't let anyone rob you of your power.
    If you forgive someone, do so because you can.
    Anyone can wrong another,
    but to forgive takes great power.
    No one can force you to love,
    if you choose love,
    no one can take your choice away.
    Love is the act of free people,
    who cannot be threatened, bound, or tamed.
    Why do you think so many lovers get crucified?

Dictators come and go, seldom lasting a lifetime.
Love lasts because love is in The Way,
Love is The Way. The Way is Love.

Thirty-Seven

The Way doesn't do,
miraculously much is done
nothing is left undone.

The Way doesn't speak,
and miraculously,
nothing is left unsaid.

If you want to lead, stop controlling so choices may abound.
Do not follow the popular mistake.
When people depend upon you,
they do not adore you,
sooner or later,
they will likely resent you
for their dependence.
Just ask the parent of a teen,
the leader of a congregation,
the governor of a nation,
dependence fosters resentment.

If powerful men and women
can ground ourselves in The Way,
the whole world will benefit.
In the natural rhythms of The Way,
people learn to be content.
Discover the arts of doing and not doing,
know when each is necessary,
all of life will fall into place.

Thirty-Eight

The ordinary keep reaching for power, and are never satisfied.
The leader doesn't try to be powerful, thus she is truly powerful.

The ordinary are always doing things, yet more is left to do.
The leader forces nothing, yet nothing is left undone.

When The Way is forgotten, goodness appears.
When goodness is forgotten, there is morality.
When morality is forgotten, there is legislation.
When legislation is lost, rulers arise.
    Traditions and rituals are established.
    Blind belief is the result.
    Chaos abounds.

The leader in The Way focuses
    on the depths and not the surface,
    on the fruit and not the flower.
    With no hidden motivations or
    self-delusions starving for affirmation,
    the leader perceives the present in perfect clarity,
    and lets all illusions go.

Thirty-Nine

In harmony with The Way, the sky is clear,
   water is clean,
   nothing is wasted.
   Humanity and nature flourish together,
   endlessly renewed,
   content in The Natural Way.

When out of harmony with The Way,
   sky is polluted,
   water makes you ill,
   earth is harmed,
   nature and humanity are at odds.
   None flourish.

Walk in The Way,
   view all parts with compassion,
   comprehend the whole,
   practice humility,
   experience a new wonder daily.

Forty

A teacher told her students, "I will die soon."
*   "No!" they cried. "Not you!"*
*   They thought because she was their teacher*
*   she was immune to death.*
*   "Everybody dies," she said. "Get over it."*
*   That's The Way.*
*   There is no resurrection without death.*

For the people of The Way,
*   death is not the opposite of life but part of life.*
*   endings do not always follow beginnings,*
*   sometimes an ending can be the first chapter*
*   in a totally new beginning.*

The Way cycles the seasons
*   spring, summer, winter, fall,*
*   then spring, summer, winter, fall.*

The people of The Way cycle as The Way cycles,
*   life, death, new life...*

Forty-One

If you are content with the poverty of others,
*   the victimization of the weak,*
*   the discontent of the masses,*
*   you are a stranger to The Way.*

If you cast out the stranger,
*   exhile the sinner,*
*   exploit the victim,*
*   then you are not living in The Way.*

If you feed the hungry,
*   shelter the houseless,*
*   nurse the ill,*
*   visit the lonely,*
*   strengthen the weak,*
*   empower the powerless,*
*   raise the lowly,*
*   knowing each one by name,*
*   as each one knows you,*
*   not in charity but solidarity,*
*   not above or below,*
*   not high and not low,*
*   but together,*
*   then you are living in The Way.*

Forty-Two

When a learner hears The Way,
*   she laughs aloud,*
*   immediately begins to walk in The Way,*
*   and soon embodies it.*
*   If she didn't laugh,*
*   it wouldn't be The Way.*

When an educated scholar hears The Way,
*   she nods in affirmation,*
*   she believes it,*
*   tells others about it,*
*   proclaims it,*
*   but does not walk in The Way,*
*   does not embody it,*
*   and does not change.*

When a dim person hears The Way,
*   she laughs aloud,*
*   and then walks away*
*   mocking it as she goes.*
*   If she didn't laugh,*
*   it wouldn't be The Way.*

The Way is foolish to the sluggish and is ridiculed.
The Way is revered by the academic,
*   professed but seldom practiced.*
The Way is foolish to the wise, is celebrated., and lived daily.
Do you see the difference?
Then you are not far from The Way.

Forty-Three

Remember The Way,
soft overcomes hard,
drop by drop,
the water gathers,
the river flows,
and the canyon is formed.

Don't fight the storm.
Become one with the water,
and The Way.

Are you burdened by regret or fear?
Try to walk on water.
If you sink, then you'll know.
Lighten up and let it all go.

Forty-Four

Fame or integrity: which is celebrated more?
Money or joy, which is more valued?
Success or failure, is one more destructive than the other?
The Way doesn't accept the common norms
    just because many people preach them.

The person grounded in The Way
    can travel as she wishes, without fear.
    She is harmonious,
    even amid great pain,
    because she has found
    a greater peace in her heart.

Though others cry for more,
    she is satisfied with daily bread.
Though others complain with each day of rain
    she rejoices in The Way things are.
Because she sees nothing lacking,
    the whole world belongs to her.

Forty-Five

You see the sky red in the morning,
*   you take it as tomorrow's warning.*
*   You see the sky red at night,*
*   you take it as tomorrow's delight.*
*   How can you read the sky,*
*   and know so little about The Way?*

Why do you speak of the dead
*   and ignore the living?*

The Way starts a fire in a word,
*   and guards it until it blazes,*
*   and then all can get warm.*

When you use The Way and are scared you'll use it up
*   don't worry for The Way is inexhaustible.*

Do you know how to arrive without leaving?
Can you see without looking?
Can you accomplish much by doing little?
*   Then you are not far from The Way.*

Forty-Six

When the world is in harmony with The Way,
  factories make clothes and cars.
When the world is out of harmony with The Way,
  factories make bombs and bullets.

The country that lives outside of The Way,
  hooks their horses to chariots.
The country that lives inside The Way
  hooks their horses to plows.

Be aware of your poverty,
  the door to the kingdom of God will open before you.
  Be aware of your hunger, then you can be filled.
  Be aware of your grief, then you can be comforted.

If you are blind to your poverty, you will lose all.
  If you are blind to your need, you will end up desolate.
  If you are blind to your sorrow, you will end up shattered.

Ask, and you will receive, but be careful,
  sometimes what you want is far from what you need.
  Seek, and you will find, but be careful,
  sometimes when you're seeking,
  your quest might take you far from the familiar.
  Knock, and the door will be opened,
  just make sure you are at the right location.
  Do not always assume you know what's best
  in your asking, seeking, and knocking.
  Align with The Way, and your choices will become clear.

Forty-Seven

Have you ever seen a perfect rose?
A perfect sunset?
A perfect zebra?
A perfect baby?
Tasted the perfect avocado?
They are all perfect, each in its own way.

Every sunrise and every sunset ,
every animal,
every person,
every moment,
perfect,
just as they are.
The only imperfection
is how you choose to see them.

When you taste sour milk, smile for it tastes exactly as it should.
When someone you love dies, give thanks for the pain.
We only grieve over people who are important to us.
How terrible if you never know loss.
Only those who never love never grieve.

Forty-Eight

Be kind to people who are unkind to you.
Do right even when there is no reward.
Love others regardless.
Why? Because you can.

When you see a little child,
think twice before you pass by without speaking.
When you see someone in need,
think twice before you pass by without helping.
When a stranger knocks at your door,
think twice before denying hospitality.
It might be God. God plays games like that,
and God gets frustrated with those
who don't play along.

People of The Way understand unity.
As one body, residents of one kingdom,
children of the Indivisible One,
when one suffers, we all suffer.
when one rejoices, we all rejoice.

Forty-Nine

The Way is like a farmer who sows his seed.
The competitor sneaks in at night and plants thorns.
When the harvest comes,
the farmer separates them out, wheat and thorns.
from the wheat, he makes bread.
from the barely, he makes beer.
from the thorns, he starts a bonfire.
All his friends gather around.
They eat the bread, drink the beer.
They are warmed by the fire,
singing "Kum Ba Yah."
That's The Way.

Fifty

When you seek knowledge, every day you add something.
When you seek wisdom, every day you let something go.

Those who think they know, do not know.
Those who think they do not know, know.

When someone
challenges you to
think outside of
the box, just laugh
because you know
there is no box.

This is The Way.

Fifty-One

If there were no books,
*   no speakers, teachers, or preachers,*
*   the rocks would still cry out,*
*   the rivers would still sing.*

The presence of The Way is as obvious as the dawn of the sun.
The absence of The Way is as evident as the setting of the sun.

Those with ears – listen.
Those with eyes – look.
The Way is all around you,
*   within you,*
*   among you.*

Those who think their family, group, or nation
*   has exclusive rights to The Way,*
*   are far from it.*

If you see yourself far from The Way,
*   don't worry,*
*   just turn around,*
*   spin 180 degrees.*
*   Like a person who spends a lifetime*
*   fighting the current of a river,*
*   as soon as you turn around,*
*   you will be in The Way.*
*   Imagine how much easier your life will be*
*   flowing in the current of The River Way.*

Fifty-Two

Those who act patient when they are not,
*   peaceful when they are not,*
*   kind when they are not,*
*   loving when they are not,*
*   sober when they are not,*
*   they are the hypocrites,*
*   acting out a role,*
*   when they are far from it.*

Those who act patient to become patient,
*   peaceful to become peaceful,*
*   kind to become kind,*
*   loving to become loving,*
*   sober to become sober,*
*   faking it until they make it,*
*   they are in The Way,*
*   growing into what they hope to be.*

Be aware of yourself and your potential,
*   enact to become.*

Clothe yourself in patience, you will become patient.
*   Clothe yourself in peace, you will become peaceful.*
*   Clothe yourself in kindness, you will become kind.*
*   Clothe yourself in love, you will become loving.*
*   Act patient, peaceful, kind, loving, and sober long enough,*
*   you will become all these things*
*   as you not only walk in The Way,*
*   you will embody it.*

Fifty-Three

"What does The Way sound like?"

The Way sounds like one hand clapping.

"What?" you say. "That is nonsense.
One hand cannot clap alone.
One hand clapping makes no sound at all."

Very well, here is a simpler answer,
to sound like The Way,
Never strike anyone with your hands.
Never strike anyone with your words.
Never strike anyone with your thoughts.
More than just sounding like The Way,
you will embody the Way.

Fifty-Four

There was a fig tree that produced fruit year round,
in season and out,
in rain and drought.
Winter, Spring, Summer, Fall,
the tree produced fruit through them all.
The fig tree never ate any of it.
The fig tree never sold any of it.
The fig tree gave it freely.

The people of The Way are like that fig tree.
In season and out,
Winter, Spring, Summer, Fall,
they produce fruit, through them all,
never selling, always sharing,
no matter what the environment is around them,
they are consistent and unwavering,
producing fruit every day, every season,
for any who have need,
simply because it is their way.

That's how you can recognize the people of The Way,
you'll know them by their fruit.

Fifty-Five

Ask a group of young children, "Who can sing?"
 almost all will raise their hands.
Ask a group of adults, "Who can sing?"
 almost none will raise their hands.
As children, they knew what singing was.
As adults, they have forgotten.

Ask a group of young children, "Who can draw?"
 almost all will raise their hands.
Ask a group of adults, "Who can draw?"
 almost none will raise their hands.
As children, they knew what art was.
As adults, they have forgotten.

Adults believe beauty is something they produce.
Children know beautiful is what they are.
Children are in The Way.
Children have the keys to gates of God's kingdom.
Do you desire the keys to the gates of God's kingdom?
 Ask a child for them.
 He or she will likely share the keys with you.
 If they have lost them, they are children after all,
 don't worry.
 The gates to God's kingdom are never locked.

Fifty-Six

If someone insults you,
consider it a gift.
If you do not accept a gift,
where does it go?
Back to the giver.

If someone approaches you in anger,
let them pass on by.
If they shower you with insults,
let them wash off you like water,
and you'll be cleaner from the encounter.

If someone approaches you lost and confused,
stay with them softly and quietly.
Their orientation will return.

If someone approaches you in The Way,
celebrate for others will come.

Fifty-Seven

The Way is paradoxical in its practice

> *Close your eyes to see.*
> *Cover your ears to hear.*
> *Close your mouth for others to hear you.*
> *Open your hand to hold what you treasure.*
> *Give to receive.*
> *Lose to win.*
> *Accept death to live.*

That's The Way.

Fifty-Eight

The greatest commandment is, "Love."
  The paradox is clear,
  love is the action that cannot be
  commanded, legislated, ruled, or forced.

Try and strong-arm someone to love,
  and you will fail.
  Love cannot be coerced.

Try and force someone not to love,
  and you will fail.
  Love cannot be stopped.

Which is why dictators
  and those who seek to control others,
  fear love above all else.

Fifty Nine

You can possess objects while you're alive
but once your objects start possessing you,
you will stop enjoying them as well as your life.
Once you forget what stuff is for,
you will become greedy.
Once you forget what people are for,
you will become dominated by your own anxiety.

Don't worry about what happens
to your stuff after you die
because after you die,
it won't be your stuff.

Just as adults don't cry
over lost dolls and trucks from childhood
in the next life no one cries
over toys they leave behind at death.

The key to peace on earth is simple:
everyone with two coats
give one to someone who has none.

People are starving while the harvest is great.
Won't someone go get the people some food?

Sixty

A country with a strong center
   can never be torn apart
   by extremists.

A country with no center
   will tear itself apart from the inside,
   no outside assistance needed.

If you need to destroy all that threaten you,
   in order to exist,
   you will not exist for long.

If you need to threaten your neighbours
   in order to feel safe
   your neighbours will become
   the threat you thought
   they might be
   and turn your nightmares
   into daytime reality.

Sixty-One

Be like the ocean
*   rivers will flow to you*
*   no force required.*
*   If the rivers do not flow to you*
*   perhaps you are like the ocean*
*   but in the wrong location.*

Descend from the high pedestal,
*   waters flow to the ocean*
*   because it has chosen the lowest place*
*   because it is humble,*
*   lower than tall,*
*   the greatest body of water*
*   is the servant of all.*

Be like the ocean.

Sixty-Two

Why do you stand outside the locked door and cry?
  Give it a knock. See who comes.
  Unless you knock, the door will stay closed.
  Unless you seek, the treasure will remain hidden.
  Do you think if you stand still the treasure will come to you?
  It might. So, become skilled at seeking and staying still.

The Way helps the lost person find his or her path home,
  and the person at home
  find his or her path into the world.
  By helping each person,
  The Way serves all of humanity.
  This is why people love The Way.

Sixty-Three

If you spend all of your life inside,
  your first experience outdoors
  will bring you great frustration.
  You will be angry the whole world
  is not 'room temperature.'
  You will be too hot or too cold with
  a small variance of a few degrees.
  You will complain the sun is too bright during the day,
  and the sky is too dark at night.
  Be frustrated if you like,
  but it's only your expectations
  that trouble you.

Each day has light and dark.
  Each week has work and rest.
  The earth has land and sea.
  Every year has seasons.

Each life has joy and concern,
  high and low,
  pleasure and pain.

Why do you expect otherwise?

Sixty-Four

The journey of a thousand miles begins with a single step.
The chip of a year's sobriety begins with a single decision.
The marriage of many decades starts with a single promise.
An Olympic medal begins with a single stroke.
This is how The Way works.
Don't focus on what you are not,
*   choose The Way of becoming,*
*   enact and you will be transformed,*
*   step out and you will arrive.*

The person with nothing to lose,
*   wins easiest.*
*   Once they have won,*
*   and have much to lose,*
*   winning becomes more difficult.*
*   This is why it is hard for the wealthy*
*   and for people with trophies*
*   to enter heaven.*
*   Once they hear,*
*   "You can't take it with you,"*
*   they aren't sure they want to go.*

Sixty-Five

Education leads to ignorance.
 The more you learn,
 the more you'll discover you don't know.

The Educated are not life-long learners.
 They see education as an arrival.
 They mark destinations with diplomas.
 They separate from others by degrees.
 The educated are uncomfortable with ignorance,
 so to pacify themselves, they label others as ignorant.
 "So many answers," they say,
 "and so many people who will never comprehend."

Life-long learners are continually on a quest
 to uncover how much they don't know.
 With every question they answer,
 they discover a thousand more questions.
 Driven by their curiosity, they are always excited,
 "So many questions," they say,
 "and so little time to explore."
 Every location, a potential classroom.
 Every person, a potential teacher.
 Every moment, an opportunity to learn.

The people of The Way are life-long learners.
 They are like the ageless boy
 who faced his own mortality saying,
 "To die will be an awfully big adventure."

Sixty-Six

The Way is a lot like swimming.

Enter the water.
Float on the surface.
   As long as you relax,
   the water will lift you up.
Become one with the water
   in the water
   and out of the water
   at the same time.
   If you try to stand in the water,
   as if you are on land,
   you will sink.
   Sinking is not being one with the water,
   Sinking is being one with a rock.
Exhale and inhale when appropriate.
   There is time for exhaling.
   There is time for inhaling.
   Confuse the two,
   and you'll lose consciousness.
   To inhale you must exhale,
   receiving requires releasing.
Those are the rules for swimming.

The Way is a lot like swimming.

Sixty-Seven

Can you wealth without experiencing poverty?
Can you feel satisfied without ever being hungry?
Can you experience intimacy without being lonely?
Can you live together if you are never apart?

Why expect any one without the other?

There is a little of each one in the other.
There is poverty in wealth.
There is satisfaction in hunger.
There is loneliness in intimacy.
There is separation in togetherness.

When you see one in the other
you are on the path of The Way.

Sixty-Eight

Living The Way,
*   you turn two into one*
*   the outer becomes like the inner*
*   and the inner is shaped by the outer,*
*   the upper becomes like the lower,*
*   the lower rises to meet the upper.*
*   Your eyes will become a single eye,*
*   a foot will become feet,*
*   images will become a single vision,*
*   and The Way will abound.*

You have a light within you
*   refuse to let it shine,*
*   darkness will encompass you.*

If you and all those with you close your eyes,
*   no matter who is in charge,*
*   you will all fall into a hole,*
*   or off a cliff.*

For people who knew you as a child,
*   it will be hard to accept you as a physician.*
*   The people who taught you to walk,*
*   will find it difficult to accept you as their leader.*
*   Heal anyway.*
*   Lead anyway.*
*   Become who you are called to be*
*   or else you will never surpass*
*   your family's lack of imagination.*

Sixty-Nine

Many go to war in the name of peace.
Many act criminally in the name of justice.
Many lie in the name of the truth.
Many dominate others in the name of freedom.
Many wrongdoings are committed in the name of righteousness.
Many acts of hate are done in the name of love.

To walk in The Way.
*   focus less on the names and more on the ways*
*   of peace, justice, truth, freedom, righteousness, and love.*
*   This is The Way.*

Can hate produce love?
*   Can war bring peace?*
*   Can domination promote freedom?*
*   Can evil foster good?*
*   No more than manure can give the aroma of a rose*
*   or a canary can give birth to a cow.*

Seventy

Your appearance does not reflect your heart,
   don't worry about what you wear.
   Your body doesn't reflect your soul,
   don't stress over your body changing.
   Do your soul work and watch your light shine.

The Way is abundant.
   To those who have, more will be given.
   To those who have nothing,
   nothing will be taken away,
   they will be given even more.
   This The Way, and The Way is really something.

Seventy-One

Know yourself, then you can be known.

If you are not comfortable with your company
   when you are all alone,
   how can you be in relationship
   with anyone else?

If you are not sleeping well at night,
   it's probably the result of not living awake during the day.
   If you cannot live every moment during the day,
   your mind will try and relive them during the night.

Don't trivialize the transcendent with clichés.
   If everything is "Awesome!" then nothing is.
   Enter moments that take your breath away,
   and let them take your words away as well.
   Be silent, and experience the mystery
   that is beyond labels.

Seventy-Two

If a child asks his mother for a fish,
    will she give him a snake?
    Of course not.
    Why then, do you look around every corner
    for a snake or some other tragedy?
    Do you think God is not a good mother?

When you are well, don't go see the doctor.
When you are hurting, don't stay on your own.

If you play hide and seek with your friends,
    remaining hidden for days,
    and nobody comes,
    perhaps it's time to come out of hiding,
    and maybe even time to find new friends.

The family The Way offers you,
    will lead you toward maturity,
    then you might be able to truly love
    the family from whence you came.

Seventy-Three

When you encounter one who is suffering,
but have nothing to give,
give them your nothing,
for that may be exactly what they need.
After all, when God created the world,
the main ingredient
was nothing.
Isn't that something?

Seventy-Four

When a mystery is revealed to you,
only share with others at the appropriate time,
do not tell your left hand
what your right hand is doing
until the time is right
and only if the left hand wants to know.

When you live an extreme experience,
there are three important words for your vocabulary.
"YES!"
"Noooooooooooooooooooooooooooo...."
and, "okay."
All three are in The Way.

Seventy-Five

If you want to lead,
*   learn how to follow.*

If you want to govern,
*   learn the art of serving.*

If you want to be respected by others,
*   start by showing others respect.*

If you want to learn to be great,
*   get in a car and drive on the highway,*
*   keep going until you come to a public rest area.*
*   Go inside and look for a person cleaning the toilets.*
*   When you find him or her working at their job,*
*   say, "Excuse me, would you teach me your ways."*
*   That's how you find someone to teach you greatness*
*   when you are walking in The Way.*

Seventy-Six

Babies are flexible.
The elderly are rigid.
The unyielding tree is cracked by the storm,
    while the flexing reed flows to and fro,
    bending without breaking.

Children love birthdays.
    Gladly they let go of one age for the next,
    one grade for the next,
    one moment for the next,
    one year for the next.

Live like a child,
    when it's time for you to die,
    let go of one life for the next.

Just because you are aged in years,
    doesn't require you to be rigid in life,
    in death, or whatever is next.

Seventy-Seven

People contrary to The Way talk about others.
    People in The Way talk with others.

People contrary to The Way walk over others.
    People in The Way walk with others.

Assume your eye is blocked by a log,
    then you will cease trying to see the splinter
    that may be hindering the vision of another.

Do not think others must become like you.
    They are no more ready to be made in your image,
    than you are to be formed in theirs.
    Each one of us reflects the image of God,
    in a distinctively particular way.
    Walk in The Way and see God
    in yourself and others.

Seventy-Eight

Faced with a starving crowd of thousands,
*   The Way takes a boy's lunch and tries to feed them all*
*   just to see what might happen.*
*   That's The Way.*

Faced with a storm,
*   The Way steps out of the boat...*

Seventy-Nine

When you are in a play, put on a costume,
assume a role, speak your part.
In your daily living, leave role taking, outfit adorning,
and hoping for applause for the stage.

If you do a good deed before others,
to get their praise,
it is no longer a good deed,
it may be quite an act.

Choose your actions and be responsible,
but not too responsible.
When you make a mistake, say,
"I chose. I acted. I did."
Accept the consequences.
If someone blames you unjustly
putting their emotion on you,
accept only responsibility for your choices.
As to the other person's emotions, just say,
"That sounds very difficult for you."

Blaming is a game that has no ending.
It goes on and on forever.
Learn appropriate responsibility for yourself
and the roles you play,
you won't be far from walking The Way.

Eighty

Years ago, someone took The Way
*   and hid it in a field.*
*   His children never found it.*
*   Their children never found it.*
*   Generations went by.*
*   The Way was forgotten.*
*   You are now in that field.*
*   Go about your daily work*
*   tilling the ground like a farmer.*
*   Guess what you will find...*

Eighty-One

There was a young boy who envied his older brother.
  No matter how hard he tried, he could never be older.
  So, he told his father, "Dad, when you die
  I'll be rich and powerful, but I may be too old to enjoy it.
  How about you go ahead and give me my inheritance now?"

Though the town thought him crazy, the father did just that.

The young boy travelled to a far off place
  where he had no brother for comparison
  and was the richest young man in town.
  He threw great parties until
  he was the poorest person in town
  and was ostracized like a foreign refugee.

He returned to his father who ran out to meet him.
  "Dad, I am no longer worthy to be your son."
  His father hugged him and said,
  "My son, worthy has nothing to do with it."
  The boy was enlightened.

The older son saw the party for his brother
  and refused to join the celebration.
  His father ran out to him.
  "That boy," the elder said of the younger,
  "is worthless and not worthy to be called your son.
  All my life, I've worked like a slave for you,
  in order to be worthy of your love,
  where is my party?"

The father went to embrace his eldest child,
  but the boy turned away.
  "Son, I love you" he said,
  "and worthy has nothing to do with it."
  The boy was not enlightened.

The father continued, "I love you
  not because of who you are,
  but because of who I Am.
  not because of how you are,
  but because of how I Am.
  Worthiness has nothing to do with it.
  Love has everything to do with it.
  Love is who I Am.
  Love is how I Am.
  Love is my way.
  Love is The Way.
  Love is the only Way.
  And the boy was enlightened.

There was a reader who read this story...

David and Carrie Jones support Haiti for The World,
sponsoring educators in Haiti
to foster a better world
for all God's children
everywhere.

For more information, go to:
haitifortheworld.org

About the Author

David Jones is a pastor and author of the following:

Out of The Crowd

Enough!

The Psychology of Jesus: Practical Help for Living in Relationship

Jesus Zens You
(Formerly published as
The Enlightenment of Jesus)

Moses and Mickey Mouse: How to Find Holy Ground in the Magic Kingdom and Other Unusual Places

*For the Love of Sophia
Wisdom Stories from
Around the World
And Across the Ages*

Going Nuts! (Fiction)

Prayer Primer

*The Moment
There's No Place Like Now*

For more information on these books,
go to: davidjonespub.com